Commissioned by Portland Summer Concerts
for Sergiu Luca

Duo Fantasy

for Violin and Piano

Duration: *ca.* 11:00

COM

T0087645

Risoluto ma scherzando (♪ = 144)   ♪ = ♪ **throughout**

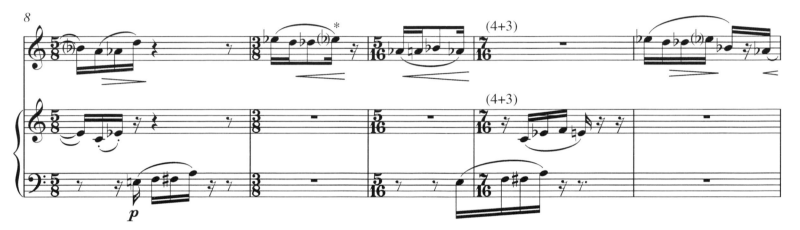

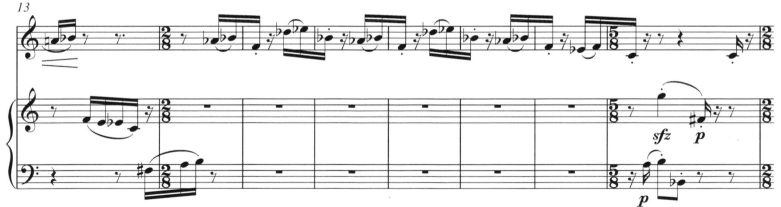

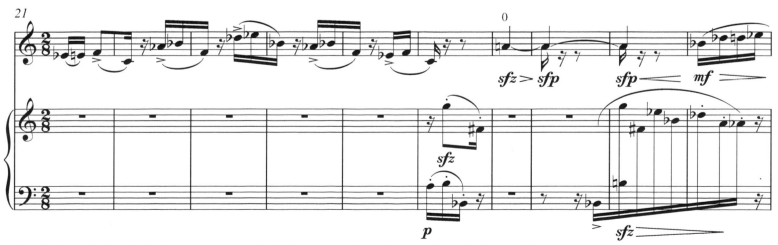

* Accidentals apply throughout a beamed note group, unless that group passes beyond a measure line, and with repeated notes unless interrupted by another note or a rest. (In sections with key signatures, policy is conventional.)

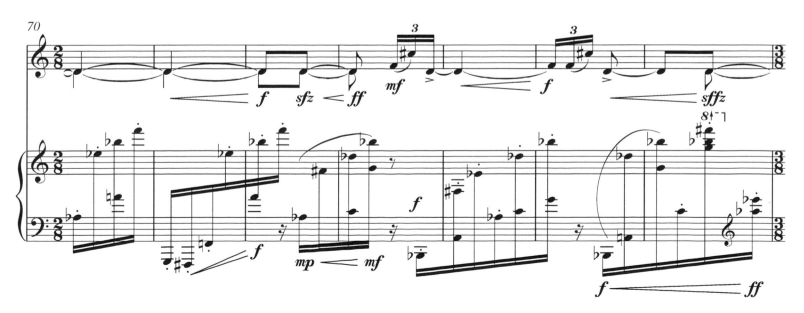

non legato, but not dry

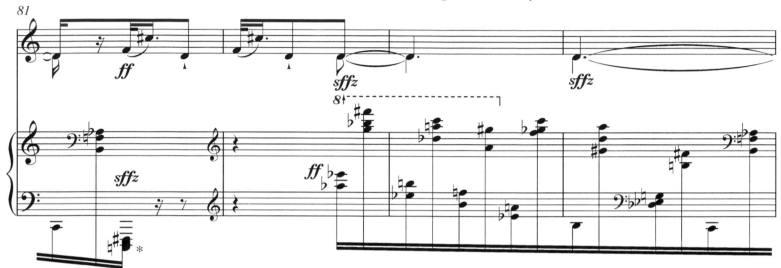

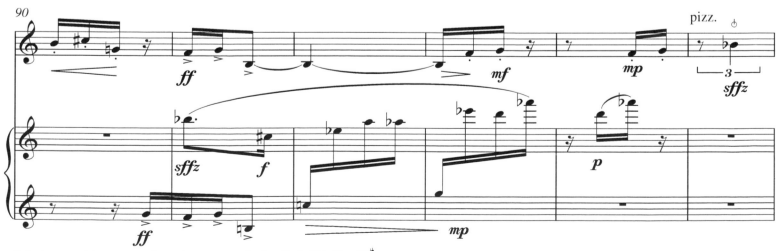

* cluster, comprising as many chromatic notes as can be described within C and F♯.

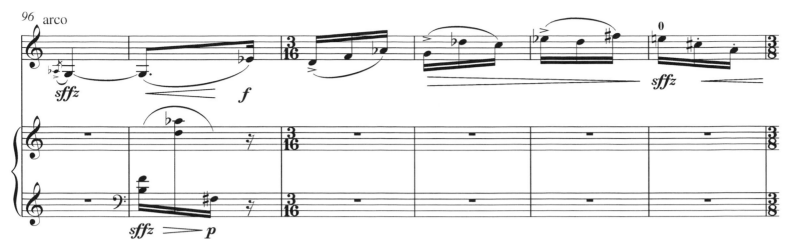

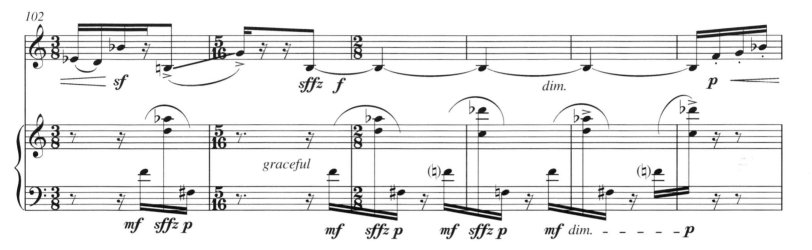

Moderato

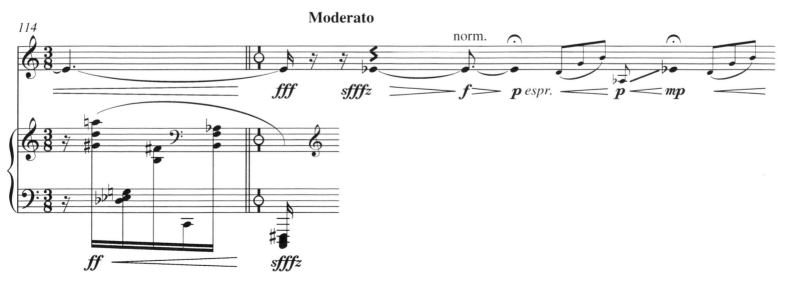

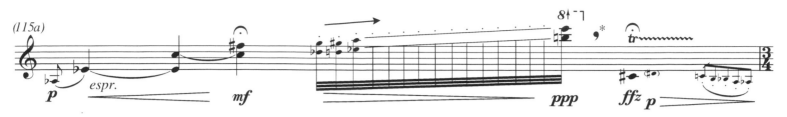

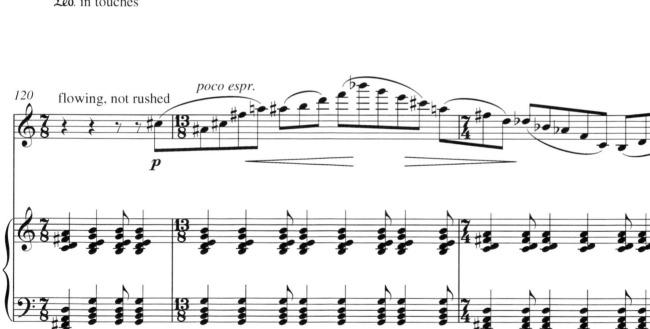

* 𝄽 𝄾 𝄿 = pauses, long to very short

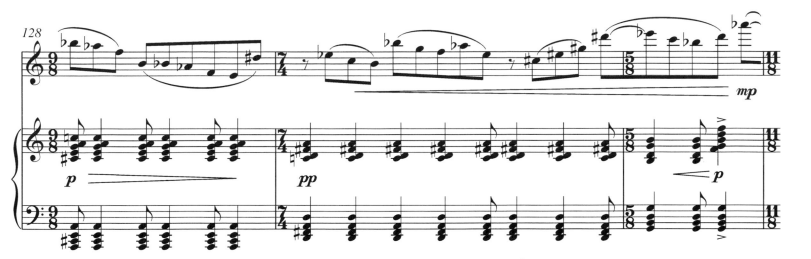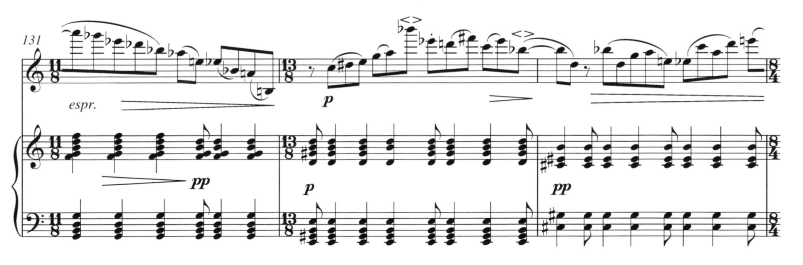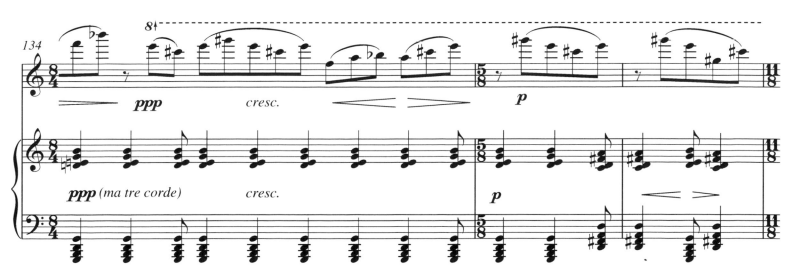

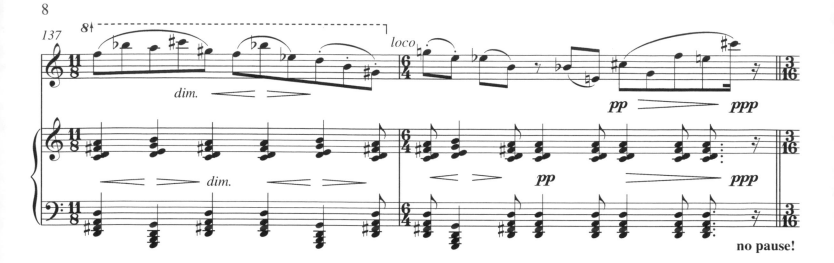

no pause!

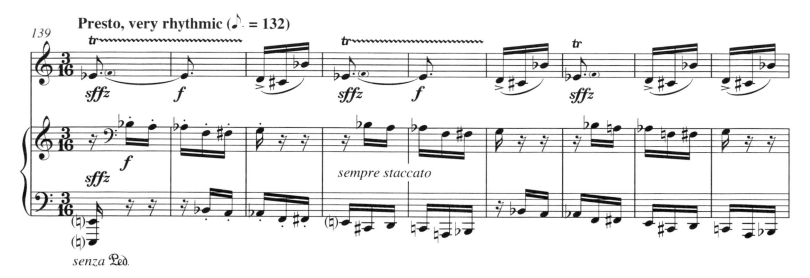

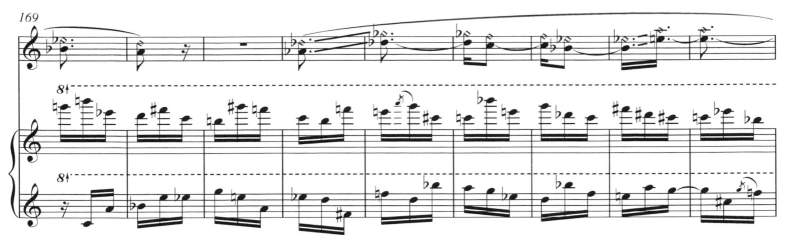

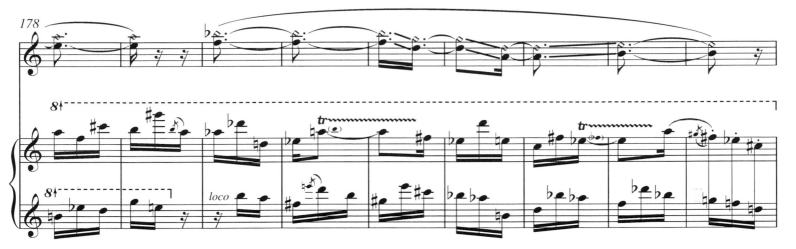

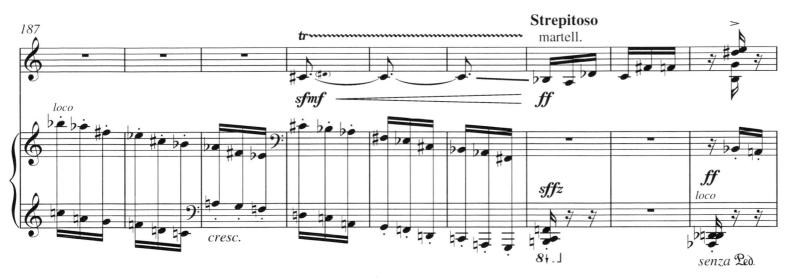

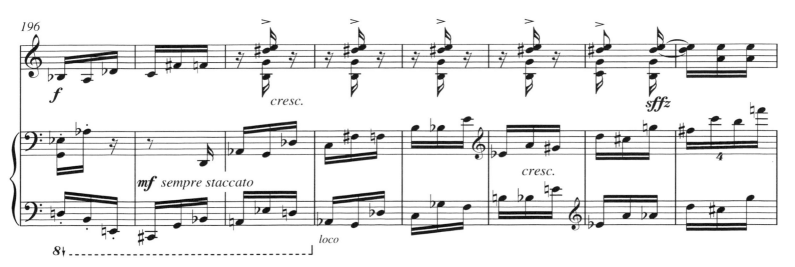

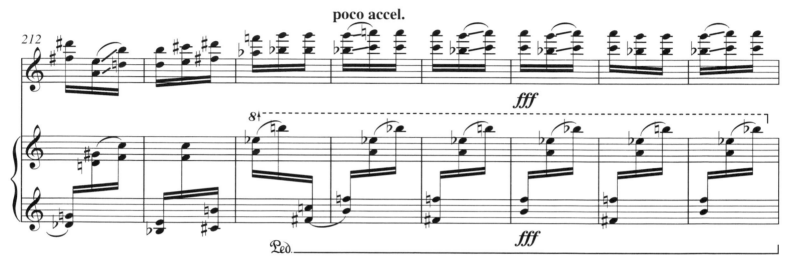

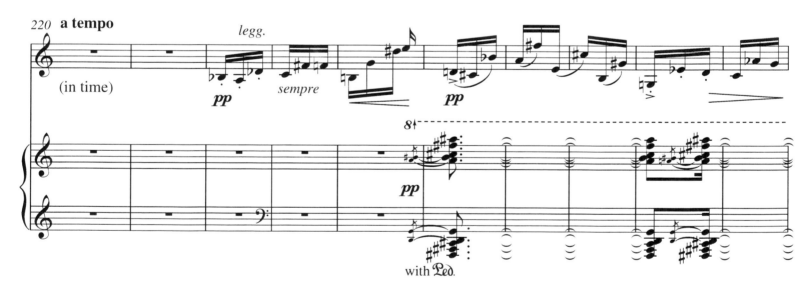

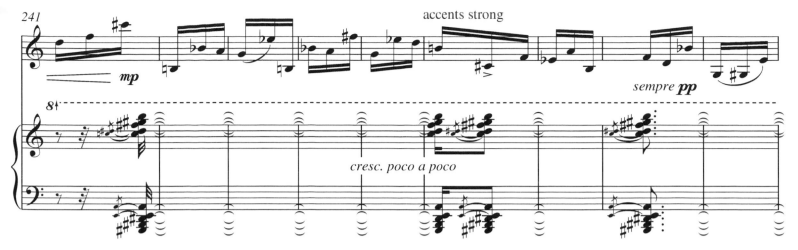

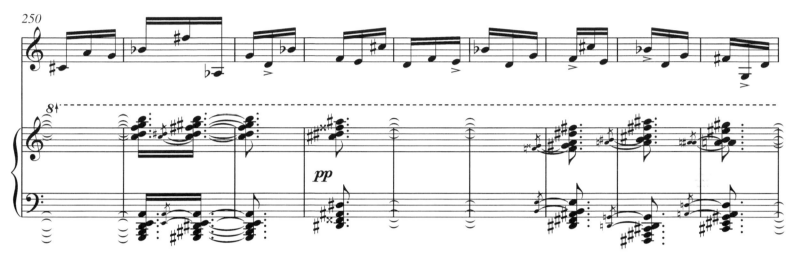

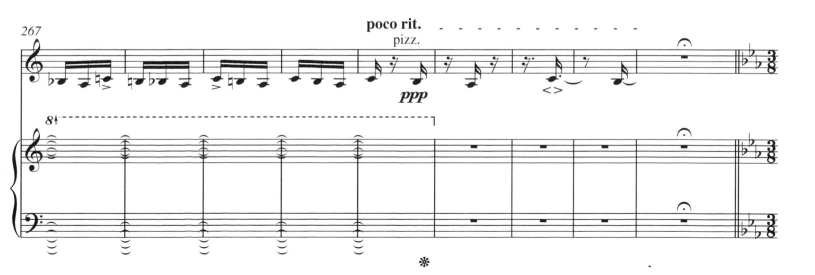

Tenderly (♪ = 100) freely, with naïveté

a little more movement

a tempo

rit.

VIOLIN

Duo Fantasy

Commissioned by Portland Summer Concerts
for Sergiu Luca

Duo Fantasy

for Violin and Piano

WILLIAM BOLCOM
(1973)

Duration: *ca.* 11:00

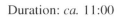

* Accidentals apply throughout a beamed note group, unless that group passes beyond a measure line, and with repeated notes unless interrupted by another note or a rest. (In sections with key signatures, policy is conventional.)

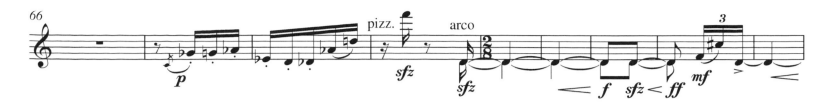

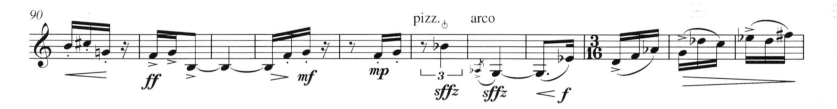

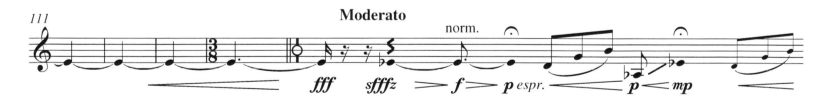

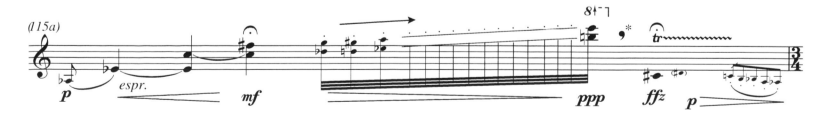

321

327

334

338

344

349

354

359

366

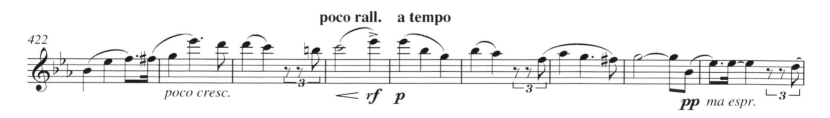

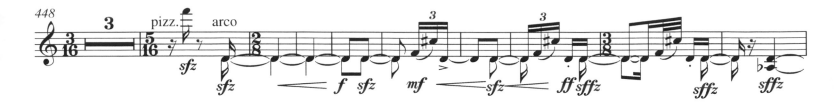

13

*slightly swung, ♪♪ should at times approach ⌐5¬ ♪·♪, but must be variable and flexible.

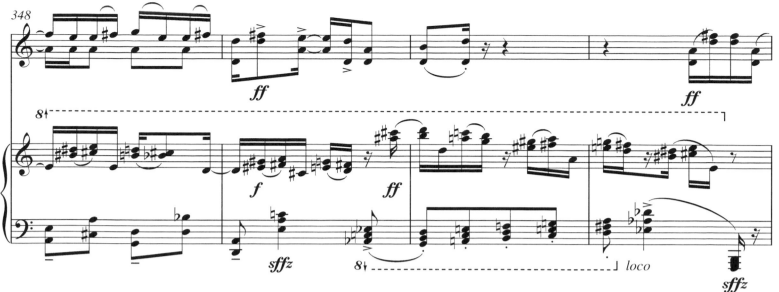

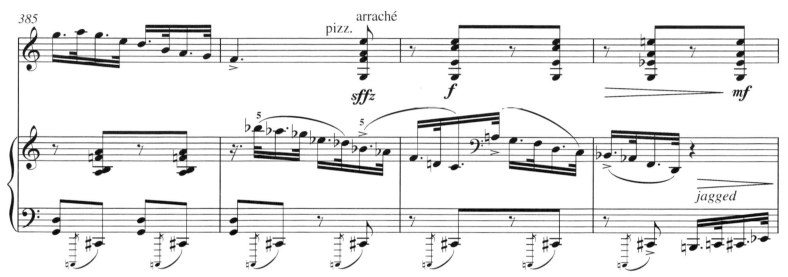

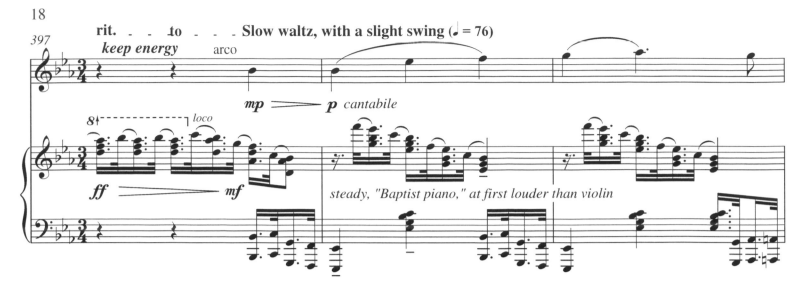

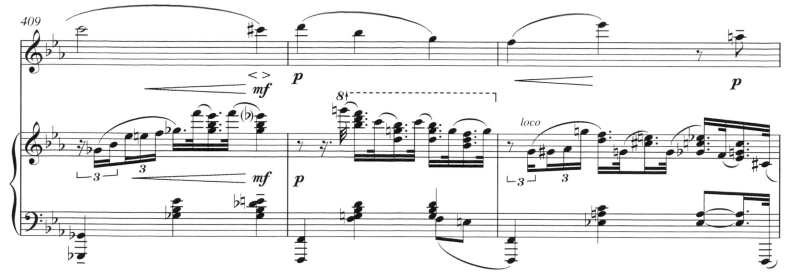

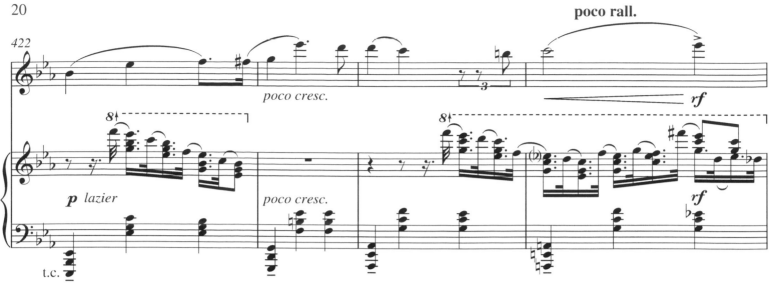

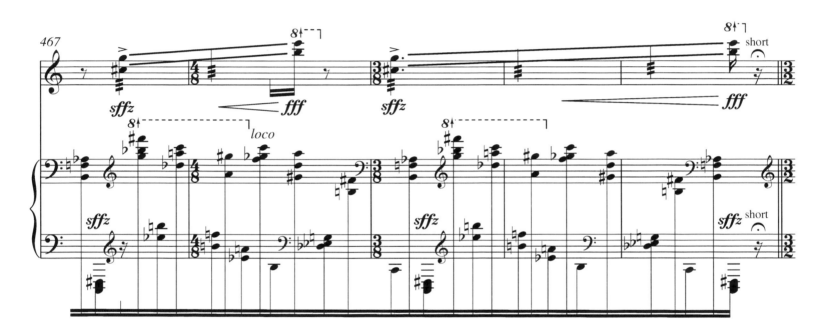

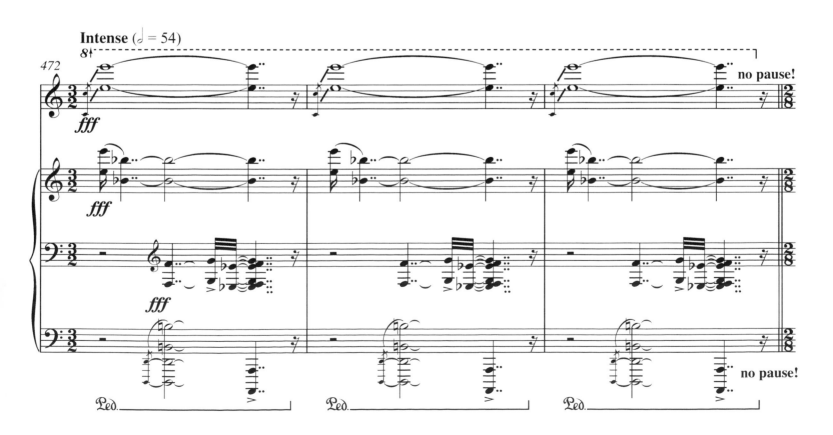

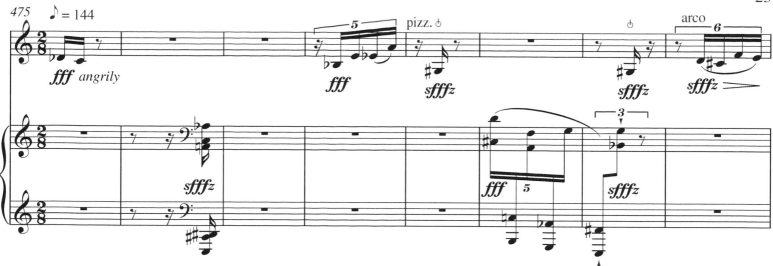

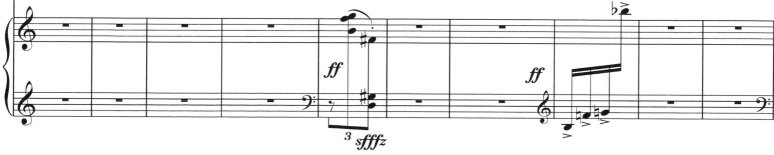

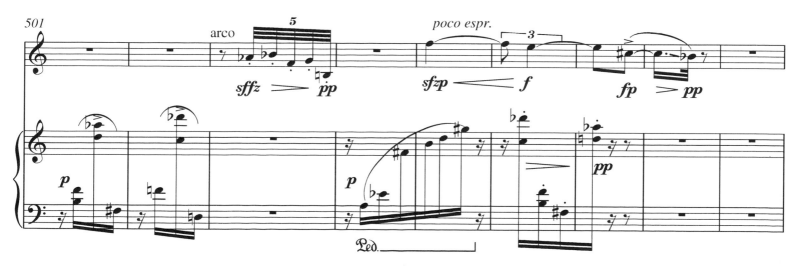

24

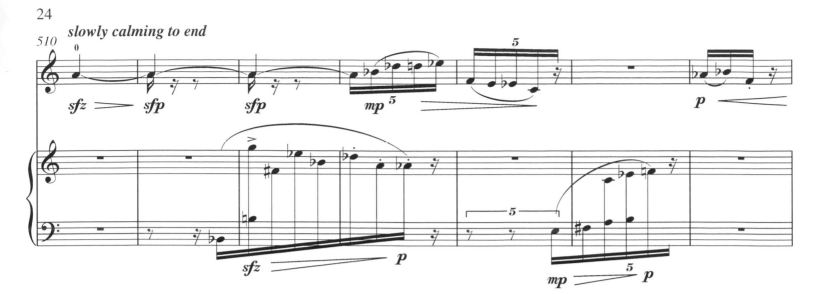

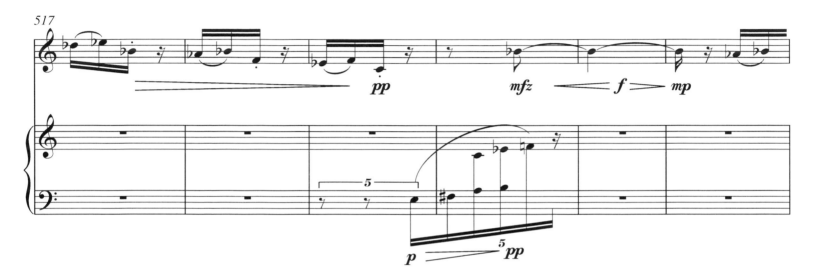

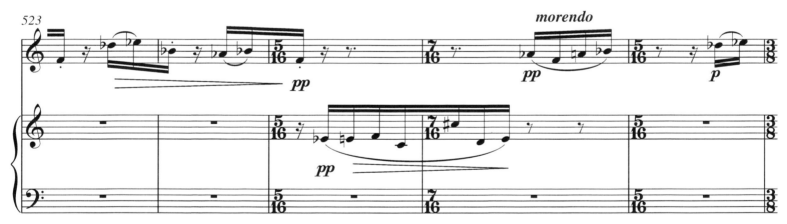

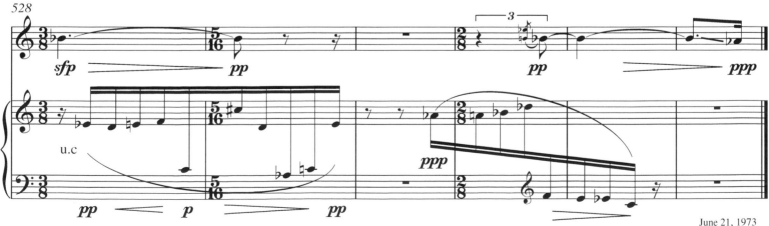

June 21, 1973
New York - Lake Oswego, Ore.